To the girl
Who has my heart
And already a book about her

Here is another,
My lover

The best way
I can describe her
Is naming her as *the Sun*

The Universe revolves around her
Everyone passes below her without any mindfulness
But in her absence
They beg for her warmth

But I always observe the vividness of the colors
Gleaming from my suncatcher
Illuminating from her

It's like we are stuck
At a stoplight
Stationed only in a crimson red
Watching other cars zoom by
While the only movement for us
Is our ominous thoughts

Kiss me
With your open mouth
Take me
On numerous trips along your route
Love me
With your whole life

When all the lights are out
Your flame burns the tallest
Illuminating a room for me
That the world tried keeping dark

What did you mean
That night when I was on Highland Street
And you said to me
" You're supposed to be
My knight in shining armor"
Was there already something more?
Or did I catch feelings first?

When you looked at me
You saw Destiny
But when I looked at you
I saw *my* destiny

Deep conversations with you
Resemble a gospel
Being in your presence
Felt spiritual
Too emotional
And the fantasies have painted a reality

More captivating than
The Duomo Di Milano Cathedral
I find myself on my knees
Praying a scripture
That gets me through this romantic rapture

Your polaroid on my dashboard
My hand pushing back your hair
[That danced in the whistling wind]
Behind your ear
Taking in the memory
You had just painted forever for me

I love you
I *really* tried not to
I tried to send you glances
A friend would
But I fucked up
And fell in love with you

I crave the feeling of being with you
You do too
Yet we stand still in ego
Neither dared to make a move

Halloween on the square
In the orange lights
Sitting on the grass
Pumpkins in hand
I kept asking myself
" Why hasn't she asked me?"
I didn't know how many more hints
I could be giving

There was something so pleasing
Of my forever being
Just you and me

She was the Midnight Sun
That existed every Summer
In Greenland
Because when I thought it was the time of day
For her to leave
She stayed in the sky
Beaming her warmth toward me

Pumpkin spice and vanilla scents
Loud laughs
And playful touches
Spiral Dinner and pastries
You always adoring me

Little did we know what was coming

Church
On a July morning
The angels were guiding and observing
While we were falling
Apart and in love

In his home,
It reeked judgment for a sin not yet committed
Suffocating us
Resulting in us parting for the first time

Told you to see me before you leave
To which you reply
Giggly
" The country or the university?"
But I really meant me

I think my silence was more than telling

Grow in love with me
Blossom at the top
Don't wilt
Graze your roots with mine
Take your time
In healing
'Cause I'll be here indefinitely

I said
A lot of things
I didn't mean
But *"I love you"*
Wasn't one of them

I am cottonmouth drunk
Craving your touch
And your whispers in my ear
Reminding me that even when I'm most fucked up
I am still beautiful and loved

My heart beats like a drum
At its fastest beat
My words play out of my mouth
Like a bass out of tune

But she
Embodies the golden-pitched harp
The softest piano
Playing to cover the noise pollution in the world

Everything thing I did
Was with the intention
Of protection
Your eyes formed waves
And I couldn't promise I'll stay
Darkness awaited me
Beyond the Earthly plane
Something saved me from beyond
What you are expecting

Through the grapevines
A bird chirped an uneasy song
The lovers cautiously feasted on the fruit
But before they knew
The vines ashen to a brown
Pulling the lovers by their throats as thorns grew
Forcing them to face Lilith apart
For biting a fruit
Before it was even ripe

Her love was as playful as the wind in the Spring
Warm like the Summer's heat
We fell like the orange-tinted leaves in Autumn
But as cold and dead as the flowers in the Winter

I love you so much
I can't help but cry

I envision a life every night
Where loving you is full time

She was appealing to every colored eye
Had the nonbelievers
Believing in the work of Christ

And to my demise
Sin lingered behind mine
And a past sorrowful enough
For my ego to die

She is the person
Lizzie Grant sings about
While the world cries
From the fresh wounds
Of loving somebody
Who hurts like you do

Through the echoes in the wind
And the brushing of the leaves
On the branches of the surrounding cedar trees
A little birdie told me
You were still in love with me
Sadly, with a murmur, I replied
" Then, where is she?"

Loving you didn't hurt me
Me being in love with you
Felt as natural as breathing

It was loving the versions of you
That had been abused
That *shattered* me

But the purest form of you?
The you that could have been?
What would have been?
Was a love I will never experience again

Tears hitting the pages of my bible
Psalm 30:5
Even Jesus felt my heartbreaking

Living just doesn't make sense
Without my baby

When you miss me
Talk to the Moon
She'll tell you enough
To make you feel my love

She watches you every night
Making sure you're alright
While I'm at a distance
Informing me through her evanescence

And when she watches
You tossing and turning
Tears gliding down your cheek
She sends you to me through my dreams

You were beyond special to me
And I got scared of the power I gave you
So I fucked up

And I'm sorry...

Don't get mad at me
Don't hide your amber eyes from me
The drugs obviously hurt you
While pumping through me
The high wasn't nearly as good
As the way you had me in a tight hold

But I fucked it up
With just one night and six drugs

When I reminisce hard enough
I can feel her touch
And the way it roamed unsure
Yet gave me the greatest comfort

3:52 am

I work in the early morning
But I remain awakened with a rosary in my hand
And anxiety in my heart
Feeling you despite being apart

You were supposed to heal
Then, come back to me
Not get with someone else
Then, move to a different continent

Your exodus
Pained me
God tried to aid me through the Red Sea
But the only fire I want guiding me
Are the ones in your eyes

Missing the parts of my day
Your presence filled
Yet missing the days
You're not the reason I lay
Tears escaping down my face

On the road
At 10 pm
With nothing but the Moon and stars
And a never-silent mind

That night
On that almost 5-hour drive

I created enough words to create a new dictionary
But when I grasp my phone
Staring at your most recent text
I have nothing at best

Why did you bring him in between
When you knew there was a lack of feelings?
Now, you're breaking his heart
Like you did mine

For what?
For you to come back to where you knew
You should have never been leaving

You never told me "I love you"
Like you did with your other friends
Claiming with them it was "meaningless"
What made it "meaningless"?
Was it the lack of romantic feelings?
Or how what you were feeling for me
Can't be told through arbitrary wording?
Or a bit of both possibly?

Are you praying for me?
Wishing on every Southeastern Asian star
Arranged in glyphs of constellations?

Your energy flows through me
As if your soul replaced my blood

If you want me,
You know how to reach me

Instead of telling God,
Tell me

I hope he knows
The poem above your bed
Is from me
About you

And the rose quarts on your nightstand
And your favorite pair of earrings
Is a piece from me

I hope he knows
I am the first
And last thought
Of your day

While he is someone
You wish away

Can you feel me
As I send telepathetic melodies
To change to rhythm of your heart beat?

Even when your hands were rough
You touched me so soft
Your voice and laugh replay
Like my favorite sonnet
Losing you was tough
But you are someone my senses haven't forgotten

Missing having someone
Communicate with me
Through looks and eyes
And when I call them "annoying"
They know it synonymous
For " I love you"

I don't know
When the yellow rose
Became red
But I knew it was too late
For me to runaway
The rose stays in my grip
As the thorns pierce me through my skin

She exists in my head as a cathedral
Both with an exterior of gold
Her eyes were beautiful and telling
Like the images on the stained glass
Her voice echoes in my head like a biblical hymn
Me feeling vulnerable in both locations

The only comfort I have
is knowing
We both are staring
At the same Sun and Moon

Over the past week
We have been reuniting in my dreams
Has me wondering if our love is beyond this reality
And you're possibly missing me terribly
But we will never know for certain
Will we?

An angel beckoned me on the terrace
Attempting me to confess
Her face blinding gold whispered
" In order to be your girl,
She'll need to fight them first
You'll know when she had sinlessly won
By keeping track of the Moon, Venus, and Sun"

I forgave you
Before those words debuted out my mouth
Before you even knew
I forgave you

Wish you made it easier
For me to leave
Shouldn't have touched my skin unless it hurt
Make me question my worth
You have too much power over me
My mind ponders
On how, when you'll abandon me
If me leaving isn't voluntarily

Being away from her
Was a moment calling for healing
Introspection and reflection
Moving on to someone who loves me better

Yet the more I find myself,
The more I find her resonating with my soul

The more I fall in love with myself
I fall harder
[For some reason]
For her

I don't think this was what people told me
Is supposed to be happening

I love you

Part of loving you
Was letting you heal
A connection I believe is real
Wouldn't last
If you persisted to paint your present
With the greyness of your past

You avoid me as if I was something you hate
When asked why
You replied
" I can't communicate"

So I began to wait

I'll wait for you to heal
But I'll first detach to heal myself
Focusing on fulfilling me
And when you're ready

I'll tell you where I'll be

You dealt with me
Gently
Even when the dance says you're not supposed to
The cold winds got too harsh
You pushed me to drown in the dark
I became the choreography you had then forgot

One day
I'll voice my vulnerability
Maybe show you all my poetry
Where you play the ingenue

I can't predict what you'll say
Can't predict what we will be doing that day
I just know I'll love you
As long as the Blackbirds sing

I can't see myself
Falling for someone else after loving you
Your presence came from pages of my mint journal
Late Sunday night
On the corner of Chestnut Street
Something about you was familiar to me
The music transformed beyond my headphones
I then knew God had something planned
All I hoped was this was something that'll withstand

Trying to get the courage
To tell you the truth
Your birthday is in less than a week
And no matter how hard I plan to speak
I remain mute

Conjuring you existence
While writing
Brings my feelings
To an internal world
Numbing the external

I can't feel Texas's July heat
Abusing me from over 100 degrees
Because I can only feel the heat I feel for you

I am aware
You're scared
And that the vulnerable conversation
Will stem from my shy initiation
I just want to transition from this stage
Where we're craving each other in our healing space

I found peace in being in love
Without always calculating the outcome
Soft like a freshly bloomed peony
Sweet like your favorite coffee

I wasn't sure back in December
Nor was I in March when we last spoke

Now, I have never been so certain
Of whom I devote myself with a lovesick passion

It was you
And it will always be you

Everyone adores Mars and Venus together
But forget about Mars and Jupiter
They bring each other stability and comfort
Within each other's orbit
And maybe if they weren't enemies with Mercury
They would have been better at communicating

When I look into
Her tea-colored eyes
I am gifted with the ability to decipher
Between the truth and lies

I awakened
To the fact
No action from me could change
How you reside in fear
And your lease wasn't up that time of year
All you did was hear
Never listen
To how much I ache for your axiom

She didn't intend to hurt me
She is not the villain
She fell victim to a home
That felt more like a prison
So once she was free
The realization that the world has more meanings
Was so scary

I miss you
I truly do
Hopefully soon
I'll be someone you [again] speak to

I desire to tell you the truth
Tell your demons to allow me to love you
They have no power
The sun flares from your heart
But the moonlight bleeds in my tears
As I attempt to translate your message
In the brightest and dimmest of stars

Although there were times I hated you,
I always loved you

Scared I'll never tell you how I feel
But here I am
Telling everyone in the world
But the one Sun-ruled girl
I ache for

She felt like she was drowning
In the darkened sea
Where the unknown reaps

Tried to grab her, making her stand
But she already had strayed far from land
Because what she felt was the ocean
Was just a small pond amongst the land

Craving to spend the next lifetimes
With you being mine
Nurturing our soul in every version
From a child to teen to our current bodies

Scared I'll never be able to tell you
I am so purely in love with you
The type of purity
Where I envision me, you, and our little family

Do I miss her?
Some moments
Then, I wake up at 6:53 in the morning
To the Sun's soft kiss on my cheeks
And it's like she's still here with me

Her image in my memory bleeds
Like the cracks in my heart
But I still won't let go
Because I love her
And will always love her

We were young kids
There was more in life to live
And more lessons to learn
So I can't be mad at a person
For not fully being someone
They're still growing to become

I love you
I still love you
And I fell in fucking love with you

For the past 8 months
I've been told to let you go

And I did
Till a realization
Crept from beyond the hidden

You have been let go
Too many times before
Your heart has constantly been left sore

So here I am
Allowing you some time
To get things right

I got close to your flame
It was too alluring
For me to remain distanced
I had slowly pooled at your feet
Like red wax melting

Drinking blueberry soda
Reminiscing the night
You sort of made me try it
Despite me not really liking it at the moment
I gulp it down
Now, it's the only reminder of your past existence

I can't pray for my forever lover
Then, not take the opportunity
When God gifted her to me
To express my feelings
Out of fear of an ending
When God is always one step ahead of me

Our initials
Are permanently in sharpie on a bathroom stall
[Definitely wasn't drunk at all]
Love the visual of our letters together
Graze my fingers across them every Saturday night
Regretting our last fight

I took down my walls
Brick by brick
Just to meet her on the other side

I hope one day
We can say this was just a stage
And our love brought reconciliation
And possibly a wedding

Looking back,
She may have fell first
But I fell harder
Nothing will change that

Your birthday
Is in less than an hour
I couldn't text what I desired
But a "Happy Birthday" will do for now

Just text me back
So we can move on from the past

Sometimes,
If I graze my skin just right
I feel her

I don't know
If you'll be in my life again

But I hope I have the pleasure
To fall in love with you again

You made me
Hate being called patient
Called me your sweet friend
Yet felt synonymous to a "fool"
But I shined like a new Moon
Going through seasons
in phases
Unaware to you

What was the reason
For us to go from strangers
To friends
To lovers
To start all over again

Rather call you my enemy
To pretend
Amongst us
There's still something

Don't know what's keeping me
From expressing my truth to you
My pride and ego possibly
But there's no point in remaining silent
When you have already left me

When your name
Went up in flames
I poured gasoline on myself till I was ash
No one really knew why I did that
But I knew I burned
To protect you
Even if it means destroying me

My love for you
Had the angels in tears
Sending me gold
When I prayed for the Sun

Sometime in the future,
My kids will read this
Wondering if this is about their mother

And that's up to us now
I wonder

Thinking about you
And all I know that remains true
Like how you loved me
And fell despite not wanting to

I made you tea
Please come back
Before it gets cold
And I have to pour down all my work and time
Down the drain

I know the intimacy
Triggered your inner child and teen
To run away
But in the time they spent with me
I hope they felt safe
And aware I loved them too

Your memories in my head
Are fading to black and white
Your voice is silent

Can you call me one last time
So I can remember your laugh again?

I may not be the one for you
But you will always be for me
So I'll age with the knowledge
You were the best
Even when you marry your husband
I'll still be imprisoned
By the what ifs
And the memories
Where I was your favorite hello
And your hardest goodbye

An angel arrived at my window
Reminding me of someone I used to know
With her
She brought courage and vulnerability
Asking " who truly is your destiny?"

And just like always
I muttered her name

No matter how hard
God nudges me
I stay in safety
Despite there not being a you and me

Just two soulmates living,
Separately

In her eyes,
Others see just brown

But not I...

I see a cinnamon tone
Like in the Chai tea you prefer warm
And if I look deeper
I see a wife and mother
Getting her kids ready on a Sunday
Eternally beautiful at even her oldest age

I love you so much
That I made excuses
For all the hurt
You unexplainably caused me

Love is a feeling
Which can mean nothing

Caring for my wounds
And showing me love isn't ruined
Was an action you refused in taking
Without actions, the feelings have no meaning

I think I got
Too close to the Sun
Now, I am covered in burns

Maybe it is best
For the Sun and Moon to stay at a distance
Only meeting in rare occurrences
Like an agonizing eclipse

I think
In a few years
When we accidentally
Run in each other again
In a different country probably
My heart will still be doing that thing

Saw him
At our local bar
We made eye contact
And maybe
I am just catastrophizing
But I think he knew everything

To save your heart
From breaking in half
You broke mine in eighths
And still, inside there's a wick
Where a flame still remains

I should be over you
<u>10 months later</u>
And you remain awake in my mind
Even in a state of slumber

Winter's forceful winds
Wasn't the only pain I felt
The attempt to dry my tears
To forget the past few years
Was as possible
As being able to move to the Moon
To avoid seeing you

Hurt my liver
After you punctured my heart
Like I was never a lover
Like there was never a part
I ever played in your life

If she didn't leave me in December,
She would have left me at the altar

Did you receive
All the prayers I sent you?

The Moon gave me yours
Just in case you weren't sure

Maybe I'm in denial
Or maybe my intuition is right
This is simply just a pause for us
In order for us to make it permanently right

Across the Lavender field,
She danced
Secretly watching me
Knowing the Lavenders bloomed
From me nurturing
With the seeds from her abandoning me

At the end of the day,
You left
And no matter how warm and comforting
Your presence was
Getting too close hurt me
And you left me lonely

Something is telling me
That whatever we are experiencing
Isn't a definite ending
Despite me again dating
Woman resembling you

I just don't understand
You fell in love with me
Then, started running
Like I did something
Yet you say nothing
I don't get what I ever did
To cause all this

I just want you to come back
Flowers in hand
Calling me from the parking lot
Telling me you need me back
As I witness from my balcony
Saying "I don't know"
But knowing I'll say "yes"

Trying to reach out
And communicate with you
Is as productive
As trying to light a wet cigarette

In a world
Of healing and hope
You would be reading these pages
Decoding my words to understand

But you won't.

You couldn't even fucking respond
To my text message

I hope you'll be able to find someone
'Cause I will
Difference is your person will not be
Better than me

Want to hear something
Extremely embarrassing?
Although we were never truly dating
I had already started envisioning a ring

I don't know when the ten of cups
Shattered to five
Or when I begged for one sword
You stabbed me with three
With five pentacles in my hand
And ten wands on my back
I'm trying to heal from my past bleeding to the present

How am I supposed to accept we're over
With no closure?
Moving forward
But emotionally and spiritually connected to her

Why do I trigger you so much?
The unadding
Entering a room where I occupy and leaving
Avoiding our eyes meeting
No greetings
Just pretending
That we never existed
That neither of us had feelings

What do you tell people
When they ask about me?
" *We no longer speak*"?
"*There are things I just refused to believe*"?
" *It was easier to end things*
Than allow someone in"?

I can't anymore
Tired of a cracked door
Letting the cold in
You should have left it locked
On your way out

Now, whatever the fucks happens
Is already written in the stars
And shown by the clouds
You can pray all you want
But your silence is where I had enough

Made in United States
North Haven, CT
04 January 2023

30626333R00072